Child Abuse, Alcohol and Cancer

I Survived It All

by

D.J. Gaynel

authorHOUSE®

AuthorHouse™
1663 Liberty Drive, Suite 200
Bloomington, IN 47403
www.authorhouse.com
Phone: 1-800-839-8640

©2008 D.J. Gaynel. All rights reserved.

No part of this book may be reproduced, stored in a retrieval system, or transmitted by any means without the written permission of the author.

First published by AuthorHouse 10/27/2008

ISBN: 978-1-4389-1691-0 (sc)
ISBN: 978-1-4389-1692-7 (hc)

Printed in the United States of America
Bloomington, Indiana

This book is printed on acid-free paper.

Chapter 1

THE SUMMER BEFORE I GOT sick, I had been golfing three or four times a week, still managing my own housework, laundry and the shopping. I weighed 126 pounds. We had some family problems, but things were getting better. Now it was time to think about me.

I had been a smoker for more than 50 years and I had known for a couple of years that I had nodules on my lungs. Dreadfully afraid of cancer, I decided it was time to go face the music and see what was going on with my lungs.

I went for a pulmonary function test and the result of that was that I have asthmatic bronchitis and I was given prescriptions for Serevent and for a rescue inhaler. So far, so good, no cancer. I wasn't sure how that could be determined with only a pulmonary function test, but I was elated thinking I was ok. Heck, asthmatic bronchitis sounded like the very least of the evils. That was in late

September. By Christmas I was feeling so fatigued that I couldn't do any Christmas shopping. I always enjoyed looking for special gifts for everyone. That year we decided to just give them money. That took a lot of the meaning of Christmas away from me.

We left right after the holidays to spend a couple of winter months in Ft. Myers, as we had been doing since my husband retired. On the trip down, I was too tired to get out of the car for anything but going to the bathroom. We ate all of our meals from drive in windows. Ordinarily, we would stop at favorite restaurants and I was always looking for souvenirs to bring back for the kids. We always stopped at favorite places to buy pecans and candies. One of our favorite things to do was to leave the motel room before dawn and watch the sun come up. We took a lot of pictures in Kentucky, Tennessee and southern Ohio. On this trip, we could do none of that. For our evening meal, after we checked in to a motel, my husband would go find a restaurant and get carry out. I was so short of breath I could do very little walking.

By the time we got to Fort Myers, I was having excruciating pain in my left arm. At first I thought it might have been the way I was sitting in the car. It continued to get worse and we were buying all kinds of over the counter rubs and ointments. I was taking 12 extra strength Tylenol a day. Nothing was helping my pain. I would have to sit up in a chair all night. I also had a lot of difficulty breathing, but I thought it was just the result of the Asthmatic Bronchitis.

Chapter 2

We didn't stay for the usual amount of time. I wanted to get home and get to the doctor. I had lost partial mobility in my arm. My feet were beginning to swell to a point where I was buying shoes that were a size and a half bigger than I normally wore. When we got back home, I was seeing a doctor on a fairly regular basis, often with complaints about my breathing. I was given a placard for handicap parking and I went for an MRI on my arm.

I was losing weight on every visit. The M.R.I showed that I have a problem with my rotator cuff. It wasn't torn, but that is where my pain was coming from. I began going for therapy sessions for my arm. I was still in a lot of pain the therapy wasn't helping.

Eventually a year was up and it was time to go back for a lung scan. This one showed that I had two tumors in my left lung. All of the trips to the doctor and I had had an M.R.I., ultra sound tests and blood work, but was never sent for a lung scan for my breathing problems. By the time I was diagnosed, the one tumor was so deep that while under going a needle biopsy, my lung was punctured. I was then admitted to the hospital I had x-rays at regular intervals to see if the lung was going to repair itself, as punctures often do. I was fairly used to having a hard time breathing, but not like this. I could not lay back and that night things were getting progressively worse. My oxygen level was dropping and finally, at 1:30 am, my daughter went out to the nurse's station to get me some help. A surgical team had to come into my room and do an emergency medical procedure. I had to have a chest tube inserted. If you ever watch the Discovery Health Program, you are sure to have seen the doctors insert a chest tube for a gunshot victim or a person who has been stabbed. It was not a pleasant thing to have to go through. They could only use Lidocane and Ativan for the surgery as I didn't have the lung capacity to be put to sleep.

After the procedure, they again took x-rays to determine if the lung was repairing and finally, after several hours, it did. I was released to go home after just a couple of days. Soon I would be seeing a doctor to see what the next step was going to be.

What I see in the mirror really upsets me. It isn't the deep wrinkles or the nearly white hair that bothers me. It's the fact that the woman looking back at me has not combed her hair in three or four days. She is in the same nightgown she put on several days ago. And she will stay that way until it is time to go back to the cancer center. That can't be me. But that is the state that I always find myself in at this time. I am so afraid that if there is a change in my tumors, I may need chemotherapy. I have heard too many horror stories and I am not sure that I would want to do that. Maybe I would just decide to let go. I only feel this way when it is time for my scans. Other times, I feel great.

When I was in my fifties, I began to think about my mortality. I decided that I wanted to live to be 74. Just 74 dear God and I made a lot of promises and I hope I kept most of them. Well, here I am at 74 and just not quite ready to throw in the towel. I guess it's back to the negotiating table.

Having cancer has made me take a long look at my life. I feel as though I have had several of them. The first was with my alcoholic mother who was very abusive. I then married a man to get away from her and he was even more abusive.

Another failed marriage and then eventually cancer, and I am still here. Those three little words, "You have Cancer" are so dreaded. I think that is the last thing anyone wants to hear in regard to themselves or their loved ones. I truly believe that in that moment, my whole life came back to me in a flash. I laid awake and thought about things that had happened years ago that I didn't think I even remembered.

Chapter 3

I WAS BORN IN THE 1930's to a seventeen-year-old girl who was already the mother of a 2-year-old daughter. Growing up with Edie was really something. She would make Joan Crawford look like mother of the year. I have pictures of myself as a very small child where you can see the bruises on my arm from where she pinched me. That was her favorite thing to do until I got older. When I was about eight years old, my grandmother sat me down one day and tried to explain to me why mother behaved the way she did. When she was thirteen, and the oldest of 4 children, they lived on a farm in southern Ohio.

THE GRANDPARENTS LIVED ON AN adjoining farm. On one particular Saturday, they were all to go to the grandparents to celebrate the birthdays of the grandmother, who had a birthday that day, and then the youngest daughter who would be seven on the following Monday. Edie was having a fit about walking up the road looking like Coxes army with all of those kids and insisted on going on before them. Her mother was getting the other two boys ready to go.

She said she would take Dorothy with her. Her mother, finally, tired of hearing her gripe, said that she could go… They would never have had to cross the street……….Some older boys were driving down the road and they stopped and yelled to ask

Edie if she wanted a ride. Without hesitating, she ran across the street, completely forgetting Dorothy, who dashed out into the street behind her and was hit by a car.

She was buried on her seventh birthday. Edie's mother never forgave her and by the time she was 14 she was already a full-fledged drunk. Her father tried to compensate for it but it was too late for Edie. She was already a lost soul.

There were two bridges that you could walk across to get to town. One was an old railroad bridge and there were huge gaps in the boards. She always took me across that one. She knew I was deathly afraid looking down into the water and she would not hold my hand. More than once, I wet my pants because I was so scared. I really got it when we got home. For years to come, I had recurring nightmares about falling into that murky, roiling water.

She could be so good when she was sober, it just didn't happen very often.. When I was very young, it wasn't so bad because we lived with my grandparents. They were mom and dad. Mother was never anything but mother. When the war came along, women were needed to work in the factories and so mother moved to a city where she worked in the steel mill. She left my sister and me in the home with our grandparents.

While living with them, my grandmother saw to it that we went to church on Sunday and I was singing in the choir. I was really very happy then. Things were fine that way for a year or so and then, for no other reason, except that she could, she decided we had to go to live with her.

Chapter 4

She had rented a small apartment over a grocery store and we went to stay with her. We were pretty much on our own and being ten and twelve, we needed guidance. She was never home. She was working shifts at the mill, which sometimes meant she was gone all night long. There were men in and out of her life. Most of them drank the way she did. Those who didn't drink, didn't stay around for very long

We would come home and often find her passed out on the bed reeking of booze. We lived in a pretty seedy neighborhood and my sister was getting quite a reputation with all of the Mexicans and Puerto Ricans They called her names when she walked down the street, but all of them liked to get her alone behind the school. Back then if you were promiscuous, it was really shameful. Today people aren't so critical of a person who has no morals. I was embarrassed by her and tried to stay away from her. She was really very pretty.

She had beautiful blonde hair and blue eyes and was just 5ft.2. As long as she was around, she got the brunt of the beatings. After one weekend of especially harsh treatment, we felt that we had had enough. We decided to run away and we took two of our girlfriends with us We talked about how wonderful our grandmother was and that if we went there she would keep us and take care of us. We decided to hitch hike there and we went to a gas station to get a map. Back in those days, all of the gas stations had maps and they were free. We went inside the station and the attendant was busy pumping gas so we were nosing around and one of the girls opened a drawer. Lo and behold, there was a metal container sitting in there full of money.

She grabbed it up and put it in her jacket pocket. We got out of there in a hurry and we couldn't believe our good fortune. Now we could take a bus to my grandmothers. We must have been really good liars. One girl was Polish with dishwater blonde hair and one was Hungarian with dark hair and big brown eyes. Betty was blonde and I had auburn hair. At the bus station security guards or some one in authority questioned us about what we were doing in the bus station alone at that time of night. We convinced them that we were all sisters and were going to our grandmothers. It was nearly midnight, but they believed us. We were singing songs and laughing on the bus ride. The walk to my grandmother's house from the bus station was just a few blocks. It was probably about 5:00 in the morning when we finally got to the house and we just walked in. The door was never locked and we woke my grandmother

She was so surprised to see us there, but before she could say too much, the phone rang. It was my mother. We were busted. Of course, we were put on a bus the next day and sent home.

We may not have been in so much trouble just for skipping school and running away, but the gas station attendant read the small article about the "Four teenage girls end big weekend escapade." He was sure we were the same girls who had stolen the money from his station. Now we were in trouble. My sister was 13 and thought to be the ringleader. Because of her reputation with the boys and because she didn't do so well in school, they decided that she would be sent to a Catholic home for wayward girls. We three younger girls were put on probation and had to report in once a week. We had to keep our grades up and not get into any more trouble. We had a curfew we had to abide by. I remember leaving the probation office and we would go into the drugstore down stairs and we would steal. We would take boxes of candy and lipstick. We did this every week and we never got caught. I have a hard time believing that we did such things because I have been so moral in my adult life and in the raising of my eight children.

Chapter 5

Now with my sister gone, I would be the only one around to take the beatings. I probably weighed about 110 pounds and my mother was a big woman. She wasn't fat, she was a big boned woman with a lot of meat on her and she weighed at least170 pounds and was 5'9." Her favorite thing was to tear my clothes off of me and lock me in the closet. One time she beat me with a yardstick until there was not apiece big enough left to pick up. I never cried and that really infuriated her. I never raised a hand against her. I would only try to defend myself but I was no match for her.

Even with all of the abuse, I still loved her and I would be so scared when I would come home and find her lying on the bed, totally drunk and passed out. Often times she had been beaten. Then she would sober up and she was as different as night and day. It never really took much for that to end.

She had for years told me that she was born with a veil over her face and she felt that she had psychic powers. She would tell me of strange experiences and when I was young I believed what she had told me.

She said she often got up in the night and went into the living room to watch her dead grandmother sitting in the rocking chair. She said the rocking woke her and when she would go out into the room, there she was. She would be smoking her corncob pipe. Don't scoff at that. My great grandmother would come to visit us for a few days and she would bring a big paper sack filled with tobacco leaves. She would sit in front of the fire and fill her little pipe and sit there and smoke. They were farmers and that was a way of life for them. She was my grandfather's mother.

When I was a senior in high school, some of the girls were buying little tubes that looked like lipstick, but it was really a color to put streaks in your hair. I just had to try it. The color was gray and I just put a few streaks in my bangs. When I was on my way home from school, I knew that she would kill me over something like this. I put some pin curls in my hair so she wouldn't notice and I planned to wash it out as soon as I got home. As luck would have it, dinner was ready and on the table. We sat down to eat and my heart was racing. I was praying that she wouldn't notice. We were nearly finished when suddenly she jumped up from the table demanding to know what I had done to my hair. I quickly explained that it would wash right out, and I was going right to the kitchen sink to do that. Before I got to the sink, she had taken out a pair of shears, tore out my pin curls, grabbed up a bunch of hair and snipped it all off. Back then you couldn't get away with kinky hairstyles and. I was embarrassed to death. I think that at the time, she was so mad, I was just grateful that she only cut my hair and not me. She screamed and raged that my hair would be gray soon enough. When she was in a rage, she was scarier than anything I had ever seen.

Chapter 6

In the fifties, we did wear blue jeans. We pegged the bottoms. But on Sunday, I always had to wear a dress. On one occasion; my grandfather had come to visit us for a few days. She told me that I couldn't go anywhere on that day as she wanted me to spend time with him. Before long, she started to berate me for being there and why was I hanging around? He was, after all, her father, not mine.

She began smacking me and she had my poor grandfather in tears. She took my shoes and threw me out of the house. Walking in the rain on a Sunday with no shoes on was so humiliating. I walked to a friend's home and prayed that by the time I went home, she would be passed out. My grandfather was going to be taking a bus home on that afternoon.

I remember her coming home late at night and getting me out of bed. She sat me down at the kitchen table and would not let me go to bed. If I tried to lay my head down, I got cracked. I was about ten at the time.

She brought home a little puppy on one of her good days. I just fell in love with him. He was warm and perky and he was all over me with kisses and that was something I didn't get a lot of. I came home from school just a few days later to find him lying in the sink, drowned………. I was heartbroken. When she came home, she said someone must have poisoned him and he was trying to get water. Even at ten, I knew what she had done. Whatever her demons were for that day, she beat them out of me.

We lived in a house with another family living downstairs and I sometimes wonder why they never did anything to help me. Back then things were a lot different when it came to child abuse or spousal abuse. People had a tendency to look the other way and not get involved.

The events are not in the proper order. I am writing as my memories come back to me. When I was very young, we had gone to one of her friend's homes for dinner. The vegetable served was creamed style corn. I piped up that I wasn't going to eat that because it had hair in it. She was infuriated that I embarrassed her. The next day for dinner, you guessed it, she gave me a bowl of creamed corn and I was ordered to eat it. When I just sat there, she began to feed me. It didn't take long for me to start gagging and puking. I had it in my head that it was really hair. We sat there for what seemed like hours.

If I wet the bed at night, which I did long after I should have, she would take all my covers away the next morning and I would have to sleep on the still damp and smelly mattress. Not only was I afraid of her, I was afraid of everything. She told me that the thunder in a storm was the devil walking and he was coming after bad little girls. Of course, I was a bad little girl because she constantly told me I was.

When I was in the fifth grade, there was a spring thunderstorm brewing. At the first thunder and lightning, I crouched down under my desk. All of the kids had a good laugh at my expense.

For my 16th birthday, she bought me a pair of roller skates. That was just what I wanted. That evening my girlfriends and I went skating and I had a great time. I finally, like all of my friends, had my own skates. It wasn't because there was no money to buy them; she just didn't want to do anything that might make me happy. I went straight home on the bus that night and when I walked in the door, she greeted me with a punch to my face. Then she grabbed me by the hair and threw me on the floor and began kicking me. The next morning you could see in the kitchen wall where she had knocked out the plaster with my head. After I got married, she would go through periods when she would stay sober and then she was very good to me. But just when I got to trust her being sober, she would, for one reason or another, be off on another binge. One time she fell down the steps and broke her collarbone and didn't know it for three days. By the time she sobered up, it had started to heal and they had to break it again and re-set it with screws.

She was living right around the corner from me and on one cold snowy night she knocked at my back door. I had a new baby who wasn't quite two months old and I didn't want her around the kids when she was drunk. I told her to go home. The next morning, she was lying on my back porch covered with snow and sleeping soundly. She could have died that night in the cold. I never really forgave myself for not letting her in.

By the time she decided to turn her life around, it was too late. She died just 3 weeks after her 47th birthday. There is a lot of talk about the cycle of abuse, but what she did to me made me love my kids just that much more. Raising all eight of them, in all that time, I only raised my hand in anger less than ten times. Once I smacked my daughter for almost getting hit by and car and it scared me so badly, I reacted by slapping her. Another time a toddler was banging on the window with his fist. I was so afraid the glass was going to break before I got to him and he got a spanking

When my sister was about 16, she ran away from the Catholic home where she had been for a couple of years. We had never heard from her There were a couple of occasions when my mother was asked to identify bodies of dead girls to see if it was her. When we finally did hear from her, she had been living in Chicago and was married and had two children. Needless to say, I married the first boy who asked me, just to get away from her. Does that ever really work?

Chapter 7

Tom was a great looking guy. Polish back ground, blond hair, and blue eyes. He had a nice tan when we met, and all the girls were crazy about him. I felt so special because he wanted me. When he asked me to marry him, I jumped at the chance I had never met any of his family and really knew nothing about him. My mother was in the hospital having surgery to remove a tumor from her stomach and we went to see her.

We told her we were going to get married and she had a fit. I knew that it was only because she didn't want to lose control over me. I was her whipping post and she needed me. We were both underage so we each had to have our parents sign for us to get a marriage license. I had just turned 19 and he was a couple of months younger than I.

We had to beg my mother to sign for us and she put us off for several months. She finally agreed. On the day that we were to go to the courthouse she stalled for so long we barely got there before they closed. She had taken the scenic route but we finally got there. Now we had our license.

We still waited for a few weeks and then one evening when we were out with another couple, we decided to go look for a Justice of the Peace. The evening we got married, he went home and I went to my home. A few days later we rented a small apartment.

Neither of us worked so I have no idea where we got the rent money. One evening while walking up town, we ran into a staggering, falling down drunk.

He turned out to be Tom's dad and we had to take him home. That's how I met my in-laws. He had two sisters who were single and one who was living there with her two small boys. It was just a small home and there was really no extra room. Still, they always made room for us when we came back to stay.

What a mistake I had made. Tom didn't work… He was mean. He didn't drink but probably only because we had no money for anything. It wasn't long till we lost our apt. We moved in with my in –laws. I was un-aware, at the time we got married, that Tom was going to be going to jail. Months before I had met him, he and a friend had gone to a party. Things got pretty wild and the girl who was having the party wanted every one to leave. Tom and a friend refused, so she called her uncle who lived next door to come over. When he tried to be forceful with them, they began to beat him up.

He was lying on the ground and they were viciously kicking him when the police arrived. They were both arrested for assault and battery. I thought later that it might have been the reason why Tom was so anxious to get married. It looked good in court. Here I was living with people I didn't even know and my husband was in jail.

I got along well with them but there were just too many living in one little house. So, every time Tom got a job and would work for a couple of weeks, we would move out…Only to end up coming back. I really wanted to have a baby, but the doctor had told me that I had an under developed uterus and would probably not ever get pregnant I was heart broken.

Chapter 8

I knew by now that I didn't love Tom, that he was just an escape for me, but I still had such a strong desire to be a mother. He was already beginning to show his mean streak. He never hesitated to smack me in the face when I made him angry. Then as bad as things were, I finally became pregnant. I was the only woman in the world to accomplish this fete. I was in the clouds I actually jumped up and down and threw my arms around the doctor and kissed him over and over again As it turned out, I had beautiful twin baby girls and I named them Katherine and Karen. They were the most precious babies in the whole world.

Kathy weighed 5 pounds and 1 ounce and Karen weighed 4 pounds and ten ounces. Karen had to stay in the hospital for several days until she got her weight up to five pounds. Mother had been staying sober from the time she found out I was pregnant.

When I neared my due date, the doctor sent me for an x-ray to see if I was going to be able to deliver the baby naturally. The x-ray showed that they were both small enough and both coming head first. That was the first I knew that there were two. Mother went shopping and she bought me the big double buggy and the twin stroller and dozens of outfits for them. We had become close and on the night I went to the hospital to deliver, I refused to go upstairs with them until I called my mother. We had no phone at home at the time so I made Tom wheel me to the pay phone so that I could call her. It was 2:00 A.M. and she knew as soon as the phone rang that this was it. We had just gone to bed when my water broke. I had an awful time getting Tom up to get ready to go to the hospital.

All of the bad in our relationship was forgotten. I wanted my mother. After hours and hours of endless pain, I finally delivered. Back then they gave you Ether. It was terrible and you didn't get it until you were ready to deliver so you suffered a lot of pain. I was cursing and crying and the nuns were really upset with me. I had always had cramps with my periods, but there is no describing the pains of childbirth. There is also no describing the absolute joy of holding your newborn infant for the first time.

The next morning I just couldn't wait for my mother to come to see my beautiful babies and me. When she did come in, she was so drunk that she could hardly stand up. I was heart broken that I couldn't share this wonderful event with her.

When someone you love is an alcoholic, there are a lot of mixed emotions. You love them and you hate them. They are an embarrassment and a cause for almost constant worry.

At the same time, you feel guilty that you aren't able to help them. You feel like you should be able to make them happy in some way so they wouldn't want to drink. You think you should fill that void in their life. If it were a husband, you may come to hate him. You would be able to walk away from him. If it's your mother or your child, that wouldn't be easily done.

I often got calls from the hospital that she had been picked up on the sidewalk passed out. One time she fell and ran a stick through her eye. I still shudder when I think of that one. About that time, she decided to commit suicide. She cut her wrists and had been pumping her fists to increase the blood flow. I am not sure who found her but I remember that there was blood all over the walls and floor.

Between my problems with her and with Tom, I was in a constant state of anxiety.

Chapter 9

It wasn't long before Tom began to slap me around. At first I was pretty spunky and slapped him back, slap for slap. When he started using his fist that was it. I lost all respect for him. With two babies to care for, I wasn't going anywhere. I couldn't count on my mother to take us in, so I stayed with Tom and just enjoyed my babies. I would put them in the big double buggy and walk all over town with them. Twins were not seen so often then as they are now. I don't think they went to school with another set of twins. When they were, much later, of course, in the fifth grade their teachers got together and decided to take the wrong twin back to class with them after recess to see how long it took the class to figure out that the had the wrong twin. They looked just alike and I always dressed them alike. It's funny now when at a family party, not having talked to each other, they often show up in nearly identical outfits.

Again we some how managed to get ourselves another apt. It was there that Tom forced me to have sex before my six weeks were up. I began to have a very heavy flow and I was feeling very weak and sick. My mother came by on one of her sober days and questioned me about why I was still in my housecoat at noon and why were the twins in wet diapers? I told her I was just tired and she soon left. About an hour later there was a knock on my door. Remember the good old days when the doctor actually came to the house? I asked what he was doing here and he said my mother had told him that I was sick. He came in and examined me and he said I was pregnant. I told him I couldn't be as I was having my periods. He said that I was hemmoraging. He told me to stay off my feet, do nothing, and some one else was going to have to take care of the twins.

Tom came home from fishing and when I told him what the doctor had said, he became very angry and accused me of just being lazy. That made me mad so I got up and went into the kitchen and did the dishes. Then I did some laundry and by then I was really flowing heavily.

I sat down on the couch to rest and Tom lay at the other end and put his feet on my lap… He said he wanted to go to his sisters and he wanted me to come along. I told him I wasn't up to it and he got mad and kicked me in the stomach and told me he hoped I would bleed so much I would drown in it. Then he stormed out the door. He wasn't gone long and when I tried to stand up, I nearly blacked out. I managed to get to the phone and I called my mother.

She called an ambulance and they arrived at about the same time she did. At that time there was no 911.

They took me to the hospital and I was quickly taken to the maternity floor. I was six and a half months pregnant and the pain was off the charts. I was screaming my head off and crying and it seemed there was nothing they could do for me. After several hours I finally gave birth to a beautiful baby boy. He weighed 2 pounds and nine ounces. He was perfect on the outside. In the fifties, they couldn't save him.

Tom showed up at the hospital and was crying like a baby and oh so sorry for everything. I doubt I told anyone at the hospital that he had kicked me. I delivered Richard in a Catholic hospital. Later in the day, a nurse stepped to the doorway and with her hands on her hips, announced that my baby had just died. With that, she just turned and walked away. The nurses and nuns treated me like a leper. I was sure later that they thought that I had done something to make myself abort.

They brought the baby in to me and allowed me to hold him for a short while. He was just beautiful with a head the size of an orange and he had perfect little fingers and toes. He had little white eyelashes and downy fuzz on his perfect little head. I decided to name him after my uncle and we called him Richard Norman.

I was taken to a room on another floor away from the babies. Being in isolation, I had a lot of time to think. Tom had really shown me what he was capable of and from then on, I was scared to death of him. We struggled over money and he almost never worked. My mother was the one who paid our rent or bought groceries. Looking back at old photos, the twins were always dressed cute and very clean. Again, thanks to my mother.

She was still going on her binges, but she was staying sober for longer periods of time since I had my babies. Those were the good times. It never lasted very long.

Chapter 10

We decided to rent a house big enough for two families and we moved in with Tom's brother and his wife. They had no children, just a dog. It wasn't long until there was a lot of friction. We argued over the menu, the water bill, and the gas bill. Still, we stayed there for several months together. Then one night after we had gone to bed, I heard my sister in law cough. Then Tom coughed. A couple of minutes later, she coughed again and then he did as well He waited a couple of minutes and then he whispered my name. Not loud enough to wake me, but enough so that I would answer if I were still awake I sat up in bed and called him a few choice names. You would have had to be pretty dumb not to know what was going on. I put on my robe and left the room and went down the stairs. A few minutes later, here came my sister-in law. She was speechless when she saw me there rather than Tom. That was the end of our living together. I insisted they move out by the weekend.

Then life went on pretty much the same as it had been. We rented the upstairs out to a friend with whom I had gone to school. She was soon to be married and her fiancé was in the service. She wanted a place for them to live when he got out in a few short weeks.

There was a cute little blonde who lived next door and Tom would come up missing every so often. I would walk around outside and call him and he was nowhere to be found. Then as quickly as he disappeared he was back. I forget what his story was, but I knew where he had been. I never confronted him with that but I'm sure he thought he was being very clever.

That summer I became pregnant again. This time I had a boy to take home with me. I fell in love with him and I would dance around the room with him to Fat's Domino's "Blueberry Hill". He looked just like his father and we named him Tommy. Things between Tom and myself just kept getting worse. He still rarely worked and when he did get a pay, he was such a child. He could blow a whole paycheck playing a pinball machine. They were popular back in the fifties. They had machines in bowling alleys, bars, and pool halls and Tom would play for hours.

On one particular evening, I had gone to a movie with a girlfriend and Tom was going to watch the babies. When I came home and walked into the house, I almost fell over. The twin's crib was against the wall where the thermostat was and they had turned it all the way up. He was sound asleep and those poor girls were drenched with sweat. Their clothes were soaked and they looked like they had taken a bath fully dressed. That just about did it for me.

I decided I needed to get a job and do what I could to get away from him.

Chapter 11

I had never worked a day in my life and had no experience at anything, but. I managed to get a job at the lunch counter in a bowling alley. While I was working there, I met Joe.

I was 24 and Joe was some where around 40. I had been working there for several months and I enjoyed my job behind the snack counter. We made burgers and hot dogs, coffee, etc. On a couple of occasions, Joe had jokingly made passes at me. I just laughed it off because he was so much older and also quite married.

And then something really tragic happened. His wife, who was only in her late thirties, became ill and was hospitalized.

After a few days, she died from some heart condition that back in the 50's couldn't be repaired. That was the first funeral I had ever attended and they had a luncheon for everyone after the service. I was appalled that people were drinking and some even seemed to be having a good time.

When Joe came back to work about a week later, I felt so sorry for him that I could barely look at him. He didn't have much to say and was just quiet and morose. They had been married for 18 years and had no children and his loss was so great to him. Over the next several weeks I really grew to care about him. Then one evening when he jokingly made another pass at me, I responded and encouraged him. We began to have a relationship even though I was still married. I was too afraid of Tom to even consider leaving him. Out of the blue, my sister came to visit from Chicago.

Chapter 12

BETTY HAD A LITTLE BOY about 7 and a daughter about 9. She was a natural blonde and when she stepped off the train, she looked like a movie star She had on a beautiful dress and as I have said, she had naturally blonde hair and was very pretty. At the time, Tom and I were living in a trailer and I was still working at the bowling alley.

After Betty had been here for about a week, Tom wanted to go for a ride one night because he needed to talk to me. He started with "almost tears" in his eyes and told me that he wanted to tell me that he had cheated on me. He said that every time Betty walked by him, she would rub up against him and she seduced him one night after I had gone to work. He said he was sorry and that he loved me so much and he wanted me to forgive him. I felt nothing but relief. It was my out… I was still afraid of him so I tried to handle it delicately and told him we needed some time apart so that I could think this over. I went to stay with a girl friend and since I had to continue working, I took the three kids to stay with his sisters. They were both single, had no children and they agreed to watch them so I could work.

Before I knew it, Tom had rented an apartment with Betty and she and my kids all moved in together. Her husband showed up and just couldn't understand what the heck had happened. He ended up taking their children back to Chicago with him. What I had to do was steal back my kids. I kept a watch on their apt. And one day when she was taking the kids to the store alone, I walked into the store and of course the kids all came running to me. She said I couldn't take them because Tom would kill her. I took them anyway.

There were some encounters with Tom. He forced me into his car one night He took me out on out on a dark, lonely road and told me that I was going home with him or I would die right there. I went home with him. He had punched me several times and I was afraid for my life. He took me to his sisters and I had to stay the night with him. He was sullen and mean because I wouldn't let him touch me. The next morning I was off and running again.

After several confrontations and a few black eyes, Tom and I were finally divorced. His affair with Betty was over and she was living with some one else. He had punched me in the mouth one time and all of my teeth were loose. I don't know how they were staying in there. I had to get dentures at 24.

Chapter 13

About a month later, Joe and I were married. He had been married to his first wife for 18 years and they were childless and Joe thought the problem was with him. After just 9 months and 9 days, I gave birth to our first child.. Being an older first time father, he was really into it. Joey was the most important thing in the world to him. He was a gifted child and later started school a year early and then in turn would graduate when he was just 16.

The first thing Joe did was to buy a bar and we rented an apartment just a few blocks up the street. The first hint of "oh oh" was when I went into the bar one day to see him and a stranger was behind the bar.. I asked where Joe was and he said, "sleeping in the back"…Passed out was a more fitting term… Joe always drank a lot, but he was a big guy and he could handle it. It would have been hard for anyone to look at him and know that he was drunk.

Eventually it became much more evident that he was drinking way too much.

Just before Christmas that year, on December 8th, I got a phone call from my mother. She told me that my grandfather had died and she was nearly hysterical. As soon as I got off the phone with her, I called my grandmother. My great-grandmother answered the phone. She told me that my grandmother and grandfather had gone Christmas shopping. It was still early, but he had wanted to take her down town to pick out what ever she wanted for Christmas. I was furious with my mother. She had scared me so badly. This was on a Saturday. On the following Monday I got a call from my aunt that my grandfather had passed away. I got goose bumps thinking that just maybe my mother really was a little psychic. I was devastated by his death. I had never lost anyone up until that time. My father was killed in World War two, but I was too young to remember him.

Two years after Joey was born, we had a little girl. I had really wanted just one little girl. I had the twin girls at home and two sons and just one little girl would make me very happy. My wish came true. She was beautiful. We named her Joanne. Joe was Hungarian and Joanne would grow up to look like a gorgeous gypsy.

At that time, we had a corner store and we did pretty well for a while. I had talked him into getting out of the bar because I felt that the booze being right under his nose was always too much of a temptation. However, our little corner store was also a beer and wine carry out and he was never with out something to drink.

It really worried me because of my growing up with an alcoholic parent; I didn't want my kids to have to go through what I did. He was never a mean drunk, just very happy and he romped around with the kids and they loved it. He would hide wine bottles all over the house I realized that the drinking was very important to him and he was not going to stop.

Chapter 14

On one occasion when I felt that he had been hitting the bottle harder than usual, I suggested that it would be a good time for him to stop drinking.

He laughed and said he needed a hair of the dog that bit him. It was a shame because he was actually a great guy and a real personality. Women liked him, but so did men. He was fun to be around, if you weren't his wife and resentful of his drinking. On one particular day, I had made spaghetti. I set the table and put the huge bowl of spaghetti on the table and a bowl of salad. Then I went out to round up the kids. When I came back in, the bowl was empty. Joe didn't know what I was talking about. He didn't eat anything, but he had a big red ring around his mouth. The kids and I laughed about it at the time, but I just didn't get what that was all about.

About this time the little convenience stores were popping up. One opened up just a couple of blocks from us and they stayed open late seven days a week. There went the business. We couldn't compete with them and eventually we had to close up the store. We moved into an apt. and though I had no real job experience except for the counter at the bowling alley, I knew I had to get a job. I could work in the evenings so that the children would never be with a baby sitter. Joe needed to be with them in the evenings. I went to the un-employment agency and they sent me to a restaurant and I began my job as a waitress. I loved it. I loved being with people. I met girls there who would become life long friends. I was in my early thirties but I had never worn make up. The gals I worked with teased me that all women my age needed a little make up so I did try it. I also didn't drink

At night, after all the work was done, the help was allowed to have a drink. At first, I would take my drink glass to the ladies room with me and I would dump my drink down the toilet. I didn't want any one to know what a prude I was.

Things at home with Joe were getting worse every day. He had a lot of good friends in town that had some connections so he got a job working for the city. He had never in his life had dirty hands and fingernails. He was still drinking heavily. Every time we went someplace, he would stop at a bar and run in for a "quick one"… I think the quick one was really about 4 or 5 quick ones because he would come out staggering.

I was still working and Joe and I were not getting along at all. He had just bought me a new car and I had been the only one to drive it. One evening when I was getting ready to leave for work, my car was behind his so he took a quick ride to the store to pick up some milk. I left for work when he got back and when I stopped for a stop sign, a wine jug rolled out from under the seat. I was so angry to think he had finished that bottle in just a matter of minutes and I trusted him to take care of my kids while I worked at night.

Chapter 15

THAT YEAR RIGHT AFTER CHRISTMAS, mother became ill and was admitted to the hospital. She had been vomiting blood. Her liver was shot and they did do some kind of by pass surgery, not with the heart but something having to do with her stomach and liver. She was doing really well after the surgery and I spent a lot of time at the hospital with her. She was going to turn her life around.

She spent nearly two months in the hospital and then she talked about all the changes she was going to make in her life.

She was just a little late with that. She talked about how she was not going to drink anymore and she was going to be a better person. She was going to be going home in a few days.

On a Monday morning I went in to spend some time with her but she was doing so well, I didn't stay long. I knew she was going to be going home and I was behind on my ironing and laundry so after just an hour or so, I was going to leave. On that day, she apologized for every mean thing she had ever done to me. Her memory of some of the events surprised me. She was sorry for things I had even forgotten about. I left to go home and I changed clothes and put up the ironing board. I don't think anyone irons any more, but back then, most of us had an "ironing day". You dampened your clothes and rolled them up and put them in the basket. I'm not sure if we had spray starch back then. The phone rang and it was one of the nurses I was familiar with from the hospital.

She told me that my mother wasn't feeling very well and she wondered if I would come back in and sit with her for a while. My gut told me immediately that something was really wrong. I never stopped for a red light. When I got to her room, she was sitting up in bed and she had been vomiting blood. She asked me to light her a cigarette. In the sixties, you could smoke in your hospital room. Then she wanted a drink of water. About five minutes after I got there, they came in and gave her a shot. She went to sleep within minutes. I think they were just waiting for me to get there before they knocked her out. Whatever kind of surgery they had done, failed. Everything in side had broken open and she was dying. I am sure she didn't know it. Even I didn't believe it. I stayed in the room with her and even though I knew she was critical, I still didn't think she would really die. I was talking on the phone to a friend who had called to see how she was when she stopped breathing. I started screaming and ran out into the hall to get help.

They shooed me out of the room and closed the curtain around her and then they came and asked me to sign for them to do a tracheotomy. I signed and then after they did that, they moved her to intensive care. There I could only spend 5 minutes with her each hour. She was hooked up to so many machines that I hated to be in there.

During her hospital stay, she had repeatedly asked me to try to find my sister and have her come to see her I did see her once in awhile. One time she had stopped to ask if I would watch her son for a couple of hours. I didn't see her again for a couple of weeks.

Betty wasn't returning any of my phone calls. I sent Joe to the restaurant where she was working and he convinced her to come and see her mother. It was too late though. Mother never knew she was there. But guess who sat and cried like a baby at the funeral? The daughter who had never come around was suddenly a lost soul because she had lost her mother. All of her friends fell for it but she didn't fool me. I think she was sicker than her mother She had never tried to make any contact with her kids in Chicago and she had since had a little boy by some one else. He wasn't staying with her either. She had let him go live with a childless couple and rarely saw him. Many years later there was a big article in our local newspaper. Her son, who had returned to Chicago with his father, was an adult now and he and his sister had sent in pictures and were hoping that an article in the paper would help find their mother. They did find her, but she wasn't interested in having a relationship with them. That was to me, so very un-natural.

After the funeral she told me how much she had hated mother and how much she enjoyed watching her die in intensive care.

Maybe she had good reason to, but no more so than I, and I didn't feel that way about her. Sitting in the waiting room between visits, you could hear mother screaming all through the hallways. She was screaming "NO" over and over and I have always thought that the devil was coming after her because she had been so evil. Everyone has heard about the light at the end of the tunnel, but there is another side to that. Some people in near death experiences see demons coming after them. The way she was screaming makes me believe that she saw some un-Godly thing

That's when the guilt set in. I should have been able to help her.

Chapter 16

I THINK IT WAS AROUND this time that Joe began to have an affair with a gal he later married. We had just bought a house on the east side of town and had only lived there for a few weeks when he decided to move in with his girlfriend. The kids and I had to go live with my x in-laws again. They always took me in and asked no questions. I was working two jobs and finally got enough money together to get an apartment.

The kids and I moved in. It was really a double house and the other half was empty. It was a real dump, but the kids hated staying with Tom's sisters. Now that they were older and could tell me things that had occurred when they were younger. When I would go to work, they felt like the cousins were mean to them and they weren't happy to be there. I recall one evening at dinner, Joey refused to eat the crust on his bread and they said he couldn't leave the table until he did. He sat there until bedtime. The next morning when he got up for school, for his breakfast, my sister in law sat a plate in front of him with the bread crusts and that was to be his breakfast. That really upset me. When she went in to the bathroom to get ready for work, I dumped the lunch she had packed into the garbage. I put the crusts in her lunch bag. She wasn't trying to be mean when she did things like that to the kids, she thought it was funny. She never mentioned what she found in her lunch bag that day.

They would also tell the four year old that they better not find any tears on that pillow in the morning.

She believed that her tears would be there in the morning and she was traumatized by it. She still mentions it every once in a while.

Chapter 17

THE TWINS WERE OLD ENOUGH to baby sit when I worked. One of my jobs was tending bar. My day job was working at a private country club and I also had to work weekends. One of my regular bar customers brought his recently divorced brother in to meet me. He was a few years younger than I and he asked me to go out for coffee. Because of the age difference, I made an excuse not to go. He didn't give up. We began to meet in the mornings for coffee and we got to know each other. He eventually wore me down and we dated for several months. I really didn't want to get married again but when he said he loved my kids that did it. We married that fall. The following July we had our first child together. We had a beautiful little baby girl. She weighed just a little over five pounds and she had her fathers big brown eyes. We named her Rae Anne. The older children all fell in love with her and 16 months later, we had a baby boy. He was the cutest of all when he was a toddler. His hair was nearly snow white and he had big blue eyes and always laughing. You never saw anyone so consistently happy. He just made every one smile.

The twins gave him the name of Remi and it stuck with him. He is nearly forty and now that is a popular name. I always consider some one having that name stole it from him

Nearly three years later I had another baby boy. The frosting on the cake He would be the last and always special to me. We named him Michael. I had been a stay at home mom for about 3 years and my sister in law came over one day and wanted to know if I would go job hunting with her. I agreed and off we went to hit all of the restaurants. Just for the heck of it, I also put in some applications.

She had a day job and was only interested in a part time waitress job because she was divorced and needed the income. I was already 40 and I thought I was too old for the job market, so I was surprised when I got a call for a job.. I was kind of excited about it but the more I thought about it, I decided that if I was going to go to work, I would rather try to get my old job back at the country club. I called a girl friend that was still working there and she had moved up to management. She hired me back on the spot. I stayed there for about 4 years.

Chapter 18

By this time, my three oldest children had become adults and the oldest daughter got married and had a baby boy. He was named Lynn after his father. Her twin followed before long and she married a young man who was in the coast guard. He was stationed at Portland Headlight and she packed up her 66 Buick and drove off. I thought my heart would break because they were going to be so far away and I wouldn't be seeing them every day. Then my oldest son joined the Marines. That was bad enough, but to make things worse, my oldest daughter decided to pack up and move to Maine to be close to her twin sister. While living at Portland Headlight Karen presented me with my first grand daughter. She would be my namesake. Then my troubles began. I was driving to work one Sunday and I felt a little congested. I thought if I could just get a few good breaths, I would be ok. I began to breathe deeply and after several times, I suddenly became very dizzy and ready to pass out.

I pulled the car over and jumped out and was gasping for air. I had taken about 5 deep breaths and didn't know at the time that I had hyperventilated. I had never heard of that. After about 5 minutes, the feeling passed and I was close to work so I got back in the car and went to work. I seemed to be fine and then when it came time to go home, I got really nervous. I was afraid to get back in the car again for fear of passing out. I began having panic attacks before they were popular. I had every possible test to see if there was a medical problem for my condition. Every test came back negative. I was fine. It was all in my head and back then the doctor told me it was "nerves". I got so I couldn't drive. Anytime I had to get in the car I would panic. Then it was a problem to be in an elevator, an escalator, and the grocery store, in a crowd or home alone. I was afraid of everything Just as I was when I was a child and so afraid of my mother. It was impossible to drive me across a bridge or to drive on the highway. I would sink down in the back seat and cringe when we went across a bridge or passed a semi. My husband could be driving along the street and I would suddenly forget how to breathe He would have to stop the car and I would have to jump out and pace up and down the walk. I really thought that if it was all in "my head" that I must be crazy. I was afraid to be alone for fear I would hurt myself. I could have been on medication. The doctor did prescribe Valium and I took just one. I slept for about 14 hours and was very groggy when I did get up. I said I would rather work this out on my own. I did just that, but it took about 4 years for me to get back to normal All of the older kids were back in town by this time and I think that did a lot for my mental health.

Things were going along pretty smoothly and I continued to work in different restaurants. I stayed in one place for twelve years and enjoyed a wonderful family of friends there.

Tommy and Joanne had back-to-back weddings in 1980. Now we had just the three youngest one's at home.

In 1986, Rae was due to graduate and Remi had begun school a year early so the two of them graduated together. Not long after, Rae Anne got a good job and moved in with friends. Mike and Remi were still at home.

I was still enjoying great health and hadn't seen a doctor in more than twenty years. The last time was when I was having panic attacks.

Chapter 19

I WAS STILL WORKING AS a waitress and in 1997 during the Christmas season we were very, very busy. I was trying to plan Christmas for my family and working seven days a week at work and often times, I worked doubles. I had run into the drugstore for something and I leaned over to a lower shelf. I got very dizzy and almost fell over. There was a bench in the back of the store where people sat to wait for prescriptions and I hurriedly sat down there. I thought, wow! I felt that it was caused by stress. During the next few weeks; I had several dizzy spells, which eventually led me go see a doctor. The cause of my dizzy spells was my blood pressure. I began to take medication for it and for the next couple of years I seemed to be fine. I had a little trouble with shortness of breath as I was in the early stages of emphysema. I wasn't surprised, as I had been smoking for about 50 years. I decided that it was time for me to quit working. My husband retired not long after that and each year we would go to Florida to spend 7 or 8 weeks with his sister.

We would always stop for breakfast and lunch and dinner. In Georgia we had a favorite spot where we would stop to buy pecans. We would take at least 3 days and a favorite thing to do was to leave the motel before sunrise so we could watch the sun come up.

When the kids were growing up, one or the other was involved in sports. Mike played shortstop on his high school team. We watched him through little league and Pony league. Lynn and Shawn wrestled and played football. Shawn was a state of Ohio wrestling champ. Joey and Remi were in bands at different times. Tom also played in a band for while. We were a family of music lovers. We went to see Donna and Beth play volleyball. Now they were grown and some were married. Donna and Rich are the parents of my three beautiful great grand children and now their kids play soccer. In the summer time the boys always signed up to play in Hoop It Up tournaments. We were always provided with great entertainment. Who doesn't like to watch their children compete? Joanne's son Jason graduated from Ignatius and got a great scholarship to attend Northwestern University in Chicago. Beth graduated from Kent and Jack; her youngest just finished his first year in college. Things were looking better within the family, but I was beginning to have more serious health problems.

Chapter 20

For the most part, I ignored the lost weight and the extreme fatigue because there was so much going on in the family. We were all so very close. My youngest son was just three weeks older that my first grandson, so my three youngest and my grandchildren were as close as brothers and sisters. Mike and Kim had been together since high school and finally got married. After about 6 months, they were happy to announce that they were expecting. My granddaughter announced that she too was expecting.

These two girls were the best of friends. We came home from Florida in early March that year as we were having showers for the two girls. We were so excited that we were going to have new babies. The shower for Donna Rae was on a Sunday and it was a wonderful, happy day. She had learned that she was going to have twins. The next day Kim went for an ultra sound. The news was not good. The baby girl she was carrying had many health problems and probably wouldn't survive. She didn't. She was born shortly after and lived for only a few hours. She died in her mother's arms. We were devastated. It is one of the hardest things I have ever had to deal with. Donna had learned that she was going to have twins, a boy and a girl. Now we had one who would have two and one who would have none. It is easier for some women to accept losing a child than it is for others. It was a long time before Kim came out of the shell she had built around herself. It was hard for them to come around to parties and family dinners. It was heart breaking.

The next dilemma, my oldest son had a nervous break down and lost his job. He had been plagued with poor health for the last couple of years and had become a diabetic. We had to pay for insurance coverage for him and help them out with groceries and rent and medications. When I would go to see him, he would be curled up into a fetal position and cry like a baby and shake all over. I was so afraid for him. It had started when he suddenly was unable to sleep. He had not slept for five days when he finally went to the hospital. This went on for months and even though he had a lot of health issues, the problem he was going through at the time was his medication. Every time he had a problem, they put him on new medication. He just kept getting worse. In turn, they increased his medication. His insurance changed and so did his doctor. His new doctor soon took him off a lot of the medication he had been taking. Within weeks he was back to his old self. He is a diabetic but other than that he is a healthy individual. The medication had nearly wasted him. You would never think he was the same guy.

His diabetes is controlled and he is back to work and leading a normal life.

With a big family, there is always some one with a problem. Rae had married and had two beautiful daughters, Rachel and Natalie. One was diagnosed as having a tumor on her pineal gland and also Dandy Walker syndrome. She was having a lot of problems in school. One of the problems caused by the tumor has to do with her hormones. She has mood swings and her medication causes her to have an insatiable appetite. Three of my daughters were having female problems and Kathy was found to have a lump in her breast. She had surgery to have it removed and we were relieved to find that it was benign.

Chapter 21

I HAD MADE A FEW trips to the emergency room for chest pain. My heart always checked out ok. Then on one of those trips, I was diagnosed as having gallstones. The evening of September 10th I spent in the emergency room. The next morning I was still in a deep sleep as they had given me medication for my pain. My daughter came bursting into my room the next morning to tell me that I was missing the most important thing that had ever happened to us. Then she turned on the bedroom TV and every channel was covering the events taking place with the Twin Towers. That day reminded me of the day President Kennedy was shot. When Kennedy was shot, we watched the coverage for days.

We watched over and over as he was shot. I think the whole world was watching when Jack Ruby shot Oswald. The saddest day of all was the funeral. Some pictures stay in your mind forever and I can still see Jackie and Caroline and little John. We ate nothing but pizza and watched T.V. It was the same during the Cuban crisis.

I was to have my surgery the following week. I had a chest x-ray and it came back normal. Several months later during a trip to the emergency room, I was found to have nodules on my lungs. That is pretty typical for smoker's lungs. I wasn't too concerned by them and for a couple of years I continued to smoke. Then I began to lose a lot of weight and I was feeling very fatigued. We left for Florida in January for our annual 8 weeks stay. On that trip down, I got out of the car only to use a restroom. We went to drive thru's for all of our meals and I did none of my usual shopping. When we got to Florida, I began to have excruciating arm pain and I lost mobility in my left arm.

Every day I was taking 10 extra strength Tylenol. I was buying every kind of over the counter rubs and ointments for pain. We decided to come home early so I could go to a doctor for my pain.

I went for an MRI on my spine and arm. I began going for therapy three times a week and it wasn't really helping. My feet began to swell so much so that I had to buy a size and ½ bigger shoe. I was so short of breath that just walking from one room to the other left me winded.

My husband had had to take over all of the household chores. He had never, ever, been called upon to clean, cook, or do laundry. Now he was doing it all. He wasn't a well man and had a double by-pass a couple of years earlier. He was a quick learner and soon was doing a good job of keeping up with the housework and cooking.

In August of that year, Remi was going to be married and they wanted to do it in Las Vegas. About 30 of the family members flew out there for the wedding. We had thought Remi was going stay single forever. He was playing in a band and having the time of his life. He had had several relationships, and was even engaged once, but he always came back home. This time he wouldn't.

I love playing the slot machines, but in Vegas, I was so tired and weak and I was spending a lot of time in my room sleeping. I was even late getting to the reception because I had to take a nap after the wedding. She was a beautiful bride and Remi was thrilled to be a stepfather to her daughter Sydney. After we got home my health problems were becoming worse.

Chapter 22

IT WAS INEVITABLE. I WOULD hear those dreaded words. "You have cancer". I had a pulmonary function test to see if I had the lung capacity for surgery and I did not. Then I. had to go for a PET scan. A PET scan can pin point cancer any where in your body. I had to fast for a period of at least four hours. When I got to the Pet Center, I was taken into a room where I was hooked up to and I.V. containing Radionuclide. I would be there for about four hours for the whole procedure. Maybe because at the time I weighed only 110 pounds, it didn't take nearly as long as was anticipated. I sat with the I.V. hooked up for about 45 minutes. Then I was taken back to the scanner. There again I was surprised to be finished in just another 45 minutes.

Now I had to go home and think about feeding about 30 people on Thanksgiving. My husband and I always do all of the cooking and baking and really don't want anyone to bring anything. It's something that we enjoy, and even with my being sick, I still wanted things to be the way they always were.

My cancer was blamed on smoking. I had my doubts about that. I can look out my window and see four of the five houses {including my own} with incidences of cancer. There are a lot of concerns in our community about the seemingly above average cases of cancer. A lot of our young people are affected.

At this point I had not yet told any one but my husband that I had cancer. I knew that in just a few days the whole family would be at my home for Thanksgiving dinner and I wanted to tell every one at the same time. I wanted to say it only once. Dinner went along just fine and then as we were sitting around the table having desert, my grandson, Lynn, remarked to me that I really looked good and asked if I had gained some weight. Then for the first time since I found out, I broke down and cried. That was the one and only time that I did cry. That was really amazing to me as I had all my life been scared to death that I might someday get cancer. I thought I would just fold up and die. But I didn't. My attitude was great. I was very angry. I felt that had I had a scan the previous year when I first started feeling so bad, I would have a better chance to survive this. Especially since I was seeing a doctor so frequently. I was scared, to be sure, but not devastated. There was a lot of crying and my granddaughter picked up her gramdad's cigarettes and tore them up and threw them across them room.

Then she left the house in tears. Every one was very somber and it put a real damper on an otherwise great day. Every one stayed for quite a while and wanted to know all about what had to be done for me.

Chapter 23

My next step was to go for a needle biopsy. The following Monday morning, my husband and all four of my daughters went to the hospital with me. I was awake during this procedure. The first tumor caused no problem but the second was so deep that in trying to get the biopsy, my lung was punctured He was un-able to finish. I had read on the Internet that if a person has emphysema, it isn't a good idea to do a biopsy. There is a greater risk of puncturing a lung, so I wasn't surprised when it happened.

I was taken out of the scanner and taken to a room where they just watched me and took x-rays at different intervals. I was having very difficult time breathing. I couldn't lay back. They expected that the lung would repair by it's self. When it continued to get worse, I was admitted to the hospital. My breathing was becoming very difficult. I was very tired, but I couldn't lie down to sleep. Lying down made it extremely hard to breathe. My oxygen level was not good.

Most of my family had gone home but two of my daughters, Karen and Rae, stayed with me for the night. My breathing had become even more labored and my pulse ox was dropping. My daughter, ,Rae, went out to the nurse's station and wanted them to do something for me. At 1:30 in the morning, a surgical team came in and did an emergency procedure right in the room. They inserted a chest tube. They couldn't put me to sleep for this.

They used Lidocane and Ativan for pain. Due to of my lack of lung capacity, I couldn't have anesthetic. If you have ever seen on TV how they do this for patients who have been stabbed or shot or traumatized in some other way, then you know it isn't something you want to have them do for you. My daughters had been chased out of the room but the one peeked through the curtain. She said later when she saw all of the blood, she was afraid they were going to lose me.

They then began to take x-rays right in the room to see if the condition was resolving. They did this at regular intervals

By mid-morning the next day, the puncture was repairing itself. I had a couple of stitches in my upper left side where they had inserted the tube. The next day, I would be going home. While in there, I was given the results of my PET scan. The news was good. I have small non-cell cancer, which is the least invasive and slow growing. I would not need chemo, just radiation.

Chapter 24

It was just a few weeks until Christmas and I had always enjoyed shopping for everyone. With such a big family there was a lot to do. The kids exchanged gifts among themselves and when every one showed up on Christmas Eve and put their packages in place, it filled up nearly the entire room. We always had a lot of fun with our tacky gift exchange. You had to find something that was really tacky and you had to put a lot of thought into. We had a lot of good laughs and this year would be no different.

On my initial visit to the Cancer Center we were shown into a small sitting room where I gave a medical history and then we watched a video. It showed the machine they would be using and explained the procedure to us. My husband and oldest daughter had gone with me. I made an appointment for the next week. I would not be starting my treatment until after Christmas

The first day there, I was measured for a jacket that would be placed on the table that I would snuggle into. It was to protect all the healthy tissue around the tumors. Then I was marked with permanent magic marker on the exact spots that were going to be zapped. I was not to try to wash these off. They would stay for all of the time I would be coming for therapy. I was going to need 32 treatments. I would be coming in at 2:00 in the afternoon, every weekday, for the more than 6 weeks to come. I would be on the table for less than fifteen minutes each time. However, on every Tuesday it would be a little longer. On that day they took films to make sure every thing was still right on.

I was beginning to get a little nervous, but I kept telling myself that I could do this. I wasn't going to be as sick as some one who was having radiation on their throat. One girl I saw who had cancer of the esophagus had a feeding tube. I would have some effects, as the radiation was accumulative, but should not get very sick. It was going to take a few days for the jacket to be made. When I finally saw it, it reminded me of a flak jacket that police officers or military persons wear. It was very heavy and they would tuck it in around me during the procedure.

On my first day they came into the waiting room and called my name. I was taken into a small sitting room. I was asked to take off my top and my bra and put on one of the little orange cotton tops that were in the little dressing cubicle. When I was ready, I would sit and look at a magazine or just chat with some of the other women who were coming or going. I was the only one with lung cancer. Every one of the other ladies had breast cancer, with the exception of the one gal with esophageal cancer. Some had no hair because they had already gone through chemotherapy. Others were about to start with chemo. I was astounded. All of these ladies sat around chatting about their cancer with me as though we were sitting around a bridge table discussing recipes. That encouraged me. It was not at all what I perceived when I thought about cancer patients. Not one of them seemed sick, including myself. They were of all age groups. One was a young mother with a new baby.

Now it was my turn to go back. My tech's introduced themselves to me and said they would be taking care of me each day.

They were wonderful. They got me all set up that first day and then they left the room. The machine made a humming sound as it moved around. In the ceiling there was what looked like a sky light with beautiful pictures of flowers. It was probably meant to distract you. As soon as the machine started whirring, I felt and electrical shock go through me. It startled me and scared me. When my techs came back in I told them that I thought the machine had zapped me and I explained what I felt. I had gone numb all over for just a couple of seconds. They said it had nothing to do with the machine. I thought then that it must be a panic attack. Before my next visit, I took an Ativan. I had them because my doctor gave them to me for our flight out to Las Vegas for my son's wedding.

I was at 110 pounds when I first started. My usual weight was about 126. I knew that I had to get my weight up. My husband was fixing little meals for me about 8 times a day. I couldn't eat a lot at one time. It was actually hard to get anything down at all. I learned what it meant to "lose your appetite" I would think I was hungry and he would fix something that I really liked. When I sat down at the table and looked at my plate, it was all I could do to force a few bites down.

It is a really weird feeling to have your stomach turn upside down at the thought of food. They tell you not to eat empty calories. I bought a lot of supplements to drink but I couldn't get them down. I could eat cheese and a few other things that were more or less bland. Crackers were good, but I wasn't supposed to eat chips and cookies and junk food The Ativan seemed to help for a couple of treatments, then every once in a while I would feel I like I got zapped again. I thought maybe because the Ativan was an old prescription and it just wasn't working. If the thought of food made me sick before, it was worse now. I would get waves of nausea on and off all day. In my journal I wrote that I felt like crap. I felt like I was hungry, but couldn't eat. As soon as I looked at the food, my hunger disappeared.

On one of my treatment days, I was taken into an office where I talked with a volunteer. She gave me a quilt that had been made for cancer patients and she asked questions about how my treatment was going and was I happy with the care I was getting. She asked if I cried every day. I said "no" and that surprised her. She thought I should cry a little every day. Approximately after seven or eight treatments, I began to see the first signs of burning on my breast. It wasn't extremely painful, but I was very aware of it.

Chapter 25

Every morning when I would get up, I would start watching the clock and I would stay nervous all day until finally time to go. I would take an Ativan half an hour before we left.

About half way through my treatments, my time was changed. I would be going at 8:00 A.M. every day. That was wonderful. I would get up, get dressed and go.

There wasn't any time for me to get all anxious about my treatment. I was marking off each treatment on my calendar and writing in my journal every day, I don't know why I was so anxious because I knew by now that I wasn't going to die in there.

I was still calling out to the techs "how much longer". It was just minutes and really no big deal. I know I was a real pain to them and I think I called out to them constantly to make sure I wasn't alone.

Every Tuesday after my treatment, I got to spend a few minutes with the doctor to see how things were going. Every thing was always just fine. I had also come to be very attached to my techs. I felt like we were best friends. Things were heading for a countdown. By the time I finished with my treatments, I was up to 117 pounds. I felt like I had made some real friends in my techs. However, on my very last treatment day, not one was to be found. I had all new girls. I was very disappointed. I am sure there was a reason for that. They just can't get attached to the patients.

The day of my last treatment arrived at last. On that day I learned that my tumors were not gone but they were much smaller. That was good news. Not the best news, but good news. We were going to wait for 6 weeks, do another scan and then see what had been accomplished with the radiation.

Chapter 26

We were going to take our trip to Florida as usual, but we were going to fly, as we were not going to have as much time. By the time we got there, I was feeling really sick. I felt worse than I had since I started the treatments. I couldn't eat and I wanted to sleep a lot. The radiation treatments had managed to catch up with me.

We took a weekend trip down to the Hard Rock casino in Hollywood, Florida. We had beautiful complimentary rooms but I was too sick to enjoy it. By the time we got back to Ft.Myers, I was back down to 113 pounds. It took weeks to gain that weight and just days to lose it all. When we left to go back home, I was feeling a little better. Still, all that was on my mind was that follow up chest scan. I had a couple of weeks to wait.

I already had the prescription for my scan and after I had that done, I waited for my appointment to see the doctor. At this point, I was more scared than I had been at any time since my diagnosis. I would always take an Ativan before it was time to go to the doctor to get my results. It was a twenty-minute drive to the cancer center and then I sat and waited in the lounge until some one came out to call me in. I think I was more nervous at this point than any time since my diagnosis. I was so afraid I was going to have to do the chemotherapy.

A nurse came and called my name and took me back to see the doctor. I weighed a whole 117 pounds. I was happy with that. After I was finally taken back to a conference room. I answered questions concerning my energy level, appetite, cough, pain, etc. The waiting was over. My scan showed that the tumors, though not gone, had become even smaller since I had the scan right after treatment. I was not going to need chemo and I would not have to repeat my scan for six months. I could stop holding my breath. It was March and spring was in the air. I was excited and looking forward to the time when I could start shopping for flowers for my garden.

I also thought a lot about being able to golf again. I hadn't discovered golf until my husband retired. Most of his friends were not available during the week. He decided that I should give it a try. He bought me clubs and I went along with it just to please him. I got a big surprise. I fell in love with golfing. I discovered that I could whack the ball pretty good. Due to my breathing issues, I would hit the ball, get in the cart and drive to where it landed and hit again. I would have loved to walk the course. I know why wives find it hard to compete with a husbands desire to golf. It is just such a wonderful feeling being out there.

Chapter 27

I TRIED NOT TO THINK too much about my health that summer and I enjoyed every day of it. I didn't think of myself as having cancer. All summer we had family parties for one reason or another. We had birthday parties for the little kids and parties just to have parties. When summer turned to fall, it was nearing the time for my scan. I would be having them every six months I have one in September and one in March. I can't explain what happens to me that last week. First it is the trip to have the scan and then it is to keep the appointment with the doctor. It never gets any easier. Each time I am just as scared as the first time. I have had to do this five times.

Last February while we were in Florida, I became very ill. I would have waves of nausea wash over me while being dizzy at the same time. This happened several times so we decided to pack up and come home early again. My scan was scheduled for March. I was so sure that the cancer had spread and again, I was a worried sick.

The day I went in for my appointment, I was again blessed. There was no change in the tumors, no involvement in the lymph nodes and every thing looked good. I walked out of there on cloud nine. I was later found to have a hernia, which could be the cause of my nausea. I also take medication for acid reflux and I am doing a little better with that.

This past January I was taken to the hospital and admitted for a bout with pneumonia. It delayed our trip to Florida and we didn't stay for long once we were there. I was too concerned about what was going on with my lungs. For the past two years, when we go to Florida, we stop in North Carolina to spend a couple of days with my granddaughter and her family. I was still so distracted and worried about the pneumonia that it was hard to enjoy them. I was concerned that my pneumonia may have something to do with my lung cancer and I might really be in trouble this time. A day or so after we were home, I went for a follow up x-ray for the pneumonia. The x-ray showed that the pneumonia was clearing up. That made me feel a little better. It was just about six weeks until scan time so I thought if every thing was ok on the x-ray, maybe I was ok. Fortunately, I was blessed again. There are no significant changes. I am good to go for another five months and three weeks. That is if I am lucky enough to still be here.

Considering my age, I am blessed to still be here. Every day is a special gift for me, but I have had a lot of other special gifts. They are in the form of my family who made all of the terrible things that I endured as a child and a young woman worthwhile. If it ends tomorrow, I have had a wonderful and sometimes exciting life. My message to anyone out there who is facing cancer, is, don't write yourself off. Have a positive attitude and don't take the time to cry. Keep your strength for fighting your battle. I believe that your faith in your God and yourself will see you through. Having a great family to go along the trip with you is also a great plus. If you think you have a problem, go to your doctor and don't stop till you get answers. My diagnosis was a year late because I didn't question my doctors.

In dealing with doctors I had been told that I had an enlarged heart. I was told I have an aortic aneurysm. Chest scans have shown that I have neither. One doctor had me on 2 medications that should not be taken together. I was on it for a year before I finally questioned it. My pharmacist wasn't aware of it because some of my meds, I get through the mail. When I called to ask about the two breathing medications being taken together, she told me that they definitely should not be. I was being double medicated and if you watch the commercials, you must know that most of the breathing aids are dangerous anyway.

When most people go to the doctor, they sit and listen to what he has to say. I never questioned mine. I wish now that I had addressed some problems that I had with the weight loss and the fatigue. When I walked out of the office knowing that my doctor found nothing to concern him, I took him at his word.

We like to think of them as our knights in shining armor, but in reality, they are just flesh and blood, like you and me and they do make mistakes……….a lot of mistakes.

I read in the Cleveland Plain Dealer today that the government is fed up with the mistakes hospitals make. A hospital is a structure. It can't make mistakes. The staff makes the mistakes. Medicare is refusing to pay for some of those mistakes. Some of the insurance companies say they intend to do the same thing. I was very fortunate in that the delay in my diagnosis didn't have more gruesome effects. I am still here and if you were to sit down and talk with me, you would never guess that I have cancer. My concern is for those people who are younger and have young children at home. How would a late or missed diagnoses affect them? I have genetics and longevity on my side. All of my great grandparents and uncles and aunts lived to be well into their 80's.

On my last admission to the hospital I was diagnosed with pneumonia. I was only in there for three days. During my stay, dozens of health care workers were in and out of my room. At the door way, as you leave the room, there is a sanitizing dispenser. In all that time and of all those people, only one was consistent with cleaning his hands every time he went out of the room. That alone was depressing to me. One who was going to be handling my breathing medications came into the room with his hands in his pockets and proceeded to put my Nebulizer setup together. I mentioned this to one of the nurses and she didn't like it.

She became very nasty with me. Not in what she said, but her mannerisms. You cannot question them. We are at their mercy. Ninety-nine doctors are great, but you have to hope that you don't get the one in a hundred who is going to make a mistake with your health. Most of the time, I feel great. You will surprise yourself with the strength you have if you are ever diagnosed with cancer. I hope you never are.

www.ingramcontent.com/pod-product-compliance
Ingram Content Group UK Ltd.
Pitfield, Milton Keynes, MK11 3LW, UK
UKHW040728250226
10912UKWH00009B/27